Religions of the World

Islam

Sue Penney

Heinemann LIBRARY

www.heinemann.co.uk/library
Visit our website to find out more information about Heinemann Library books.

To order:

 Phone 44 (0) 1865 888066
 Send a fax to 44 (0) 1865 314091
Visit the Heinemann Bookshop at www.heinemann.co.uk/library to browse our catalogue and order online.

First published in Great Britain by Heinemann Library, Halley Court, Jordan Hill, Oxford OX2 8EJ
a division of Reed Educational and Professional Publishing Ltd.
Heinemann is a registered trademark of Reed Educational & Professional Publishing Ltd.

OXFORD MELBOURNE AUCKLAND JOHANNESBURG BLANTYRE
GABORONE IBADAN PORTSMOUTH (NH) USA CHICAGO

Designed by Ken Vail Graphic Design
Originated by Universal
Printed by Wing King Tong in Hong Kong.

ISBN 0 431 14952 6
06 05 04 03 02
10 9 8 7 6 5 4 3 2 1

British Library Cataloguing in Publication Data

Penney, Sue
Islam. – (Religions of the world)
1. Islam – Juvenile literature
1.Title
297

Acknowledgements
The Publishers would like to thank the following for permission to reproduce copyright material:
Roman transliteration of the Holy Qu'ran, with English translation, Abdullah Yusuf Ali, Sh Muhammad Ashraf Publishers, Pakistan.

The Publishers would like to thank the following for permission to reproduce photographs:
Ancient Art and Architecture p.35; Carlos Reyes-Manzo/Andes Press Agency, p.40; Circa Photo Library/William Holtby, pp.25, 31, 32, 41; Photoedit, p.18, Stock Boston, p.42. All other photos: Peter Sanders

Cover photograph reproduced with permission of Circa Photo Library/William Holtby.

Our thanks to Philip Emmett for his comments in the preparation of this book.

Every effort has been made to contact copyright holders of any material reproduced in this book. Any omissions will be rectified in subsequent printings if notice is given to the Publisher.

Words appearing in the text in bold, **like this**, are explained in the Glossary.

Contents

Dates: in this book, dates are followed by the letters BCE (Before Common Era) or CE (Common Era). This is instead of using BC (Before Christ) and AD (*Anno Domini*, meaning In the year of our Lord), which is a Christian system. The date numbers are the same in both systems.

Introducing Islam

Islam is the religion of people called Muslims. Islam began in the part of the world now called the Middle East. Today there are Muslims living in almost every country in the world.

What do Muslims believe?

This girl is a Muslim who comes from a country in Africa.

Muslims believe that there is one God. They call God **Allah**. They believe that Allah is **eternal**. This means that he was never born and he will never die. Allah made everything, and he knows and sees everything, too. He cares about what he made. Because Allah made them and loves them, human beings should worship and love him. Muslims believe that all people should try to live in the right way. Allah expects this, and he cares more about how hard people try to do this than how well they succeed.

The prophet Muhammad

Muslims believe that human beings know about Allah because he sent **prophets** to earth to tell them. They believe there have been thousands of prophets over thousands of years. The last and most important prophet was a man called Muhammad. He was born in the country now called Saudi Arabia in 570 CE. Muslims believe that Muhammad was given messages from Allah. They were given to him by an **angel** called Jibril. These messages were collected together to form the **Qur'an**. This is the Muslims' holy book.

The Shahadah

Muslims believe that their most important beliefs can be summed up in a sentence called the **Shahadah**. In English, this is: 'There is no God except Allah, and Muhammad is the messenger of Allah.' Muslims repeat the Shahadah every night and every morning, and when they pray.

This picture is made up of the Arabic letters which spell the Shahadah.

Islam fact check
- *Muslims believe in one God whose name is Allah.*
- *Muslims follow the teachings of a prophet called Muhammad.*
- *The most important Muslim teachings are in their holy book, called the Qur'an.*
- *The Qur'an is written in **Arabic**, the language which Muhammad spoke.*
- *The place where Muslims meet for worship is usually called a **mosque**.*
- *There are about 1.3 billion Muslims living in the world today. About 1.5 million Muslims live in the UK.*

The life of Muhammad

▲ *Camel traders today still live and work in much the same way as Muhammad did.*

Muhammad's early life

Muhammad was born in a city called Makkah, in the country now called Saudi Arabia. He was probably born in the year 570 CE. Muhammad's father died before he was born, and when he was only six years old his mother died. His grandfather, and later his uncle, looked after Muhammad until he grew up.

You can find the places mentioned in this book on the map on page 44.

Muhammad's uncle was a trader, who used to buy and sell goods. Muhammad began working for him. Muhammad was honest and good, and people respected him. After some years, Muhammad began working for another trader, a woman called Khadijah. When Muhammad was 25, he and Khadijah were married. They were very happy.

Muhammad's visions

Muhammad became worried about things he saw in the city of Makkah. People were not living good lives. There was fighting and drinking, and poor people were treated badly. Many people worshipped **idols**, which were statues made of wood and stone. Muhammad was sure that these things were wrong. He began going to a cave outside the city where he could spend time alone to think and to pray.

*The Great **Mosque** in Makkah today. The mountain in the background is where Muhammad went to pray.*

One night, when he was about 40 years old, Muhammad was praying in the cave. Suddenly, he saw the **angel** Jibril (sometimes known as Gabriel). Jibril showed Muhammad some writing in burning letters and told him to read it. This writing was a message from **Allah**. Jibril said, 'Muhammad! You are Allah's messenger!'

Muhammad was very frightened. He returned home, and told Khadijah what had happened. After some time, Muhammad began teaching in Makkah. Later, he moved to a town called Madinah.

Prophets

*A **prophet** is someone who brings messages from God. Islam teaches that since the beginning of the world there have been 124,000 prophets. These prophets include Adam – the first man – and Abraham, Moses and Jesus. (Muslims call them Ibrahim, Musa and Isa.) Islam teaches that Muhammad was the last prophet. His messages were the words of Allah and will never be changed.*

The hijrah

▲ *The Mosque of the Prophet in Madinah today.*

The **hijrah** is the name given to the journey which Muhammad made from Makkah to Madinah in 622 CE. People from Madinah had heard Muhammad teach in Makkah, and they wanted him to come and teach them, too. But the journey was dangerous. Muhammad had made many enemies in Makkah because of his teaching. People in Makkah did not like being told that the way they lived was wrong. The road across the desert to Madinah was lonely, and his enemies could easily have killed him. There are many stories which tell how **Allah** protected Muhammad and his family on the journey.

You can find the places mentioned in this book on the map on page 44.

When he arrived in Madinah, Muhammad was treated with great respect. He became a leader of the town. People listened to him and followed his teaching. Muhammad worked in Madinah for 10 years. During this time, the people of Makkah became very unhappy that the new religion Muhammad was teaching about was getting stronger and stronger. The people of Makkah began making life difficult for the people of Madinah, and there were many fights and battles.

Makkah becomes a holy city

In 628 CE, Muhammad received a message from Allah telling him that he would return to Makkah. Muhammad went, and he made peace with the people of Makkah. Muhammad then returned to Madinah.

Two years later, the trouble started again. Muhammad returned once again to Makkah, this time with an army of 10,000 men. The people of Makkah accepted the new religion, Islam, without a fight. All the **idols** were taken out of the city and burnt. Makkah became a holy city. Only Muslims were allowed to go there. This rule still applies today.

Muhammad's death

After this, Muhammad went back to Madinah, and worked there for another two years. In 632 CE, he caught a fever, and he died on 7 June. His body was buried in the house where he lived. A beautiful **mosque** called the Mosque of the Prophet was built over the site. Today, this is one of the most important mosques in the world.

'Peace be upon him'

*Muslims only worship Allah. However, they treat the names of Muhammed and all the **prophets** with great respect. Whenever Muslims say the name of Muhammad, they add the words: 'Peace and blessings of Allah upon him.' When they say the name of one of the other prophets, they add: 'Peace be upon him.' In **Arabic**, the language of Islam, these words can be written in a special way:*

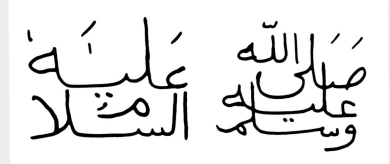

'Peace be upon him.'

'Peace and blessings of Allah upon him.'

The early days of Islam

The first four khalifahs

When Muhammad died, his followers had to choose a new leader. There were two possible choices. One, Ali, was married to Muhammad's daughter. The other, Abu Bakr, had been one of Muhammad's closest friends. At last, Abu Bakr was chosen to become the first **khalifah** (leader).

Abu Bakr was khalifah for two years. Then he died, and a man called Umar took over. Umar was khalifah for 10 years. After he died, a man called Uthman became the next khalifah. Twelve years later, Ali – Muhammad's son-in-law – became khalifah. This was the man that many Muslims had wanted to take over from Muhammad 24 years earlier.

What did the first khalifahs do?

During Muhammad's life, almost all of the country we call Saudi Arabia became Muslim. While Abu Bakr was khalifah, Islam spread into nearby countries. Over the next few years, Islam spread through the countries of Syria and Palestine.

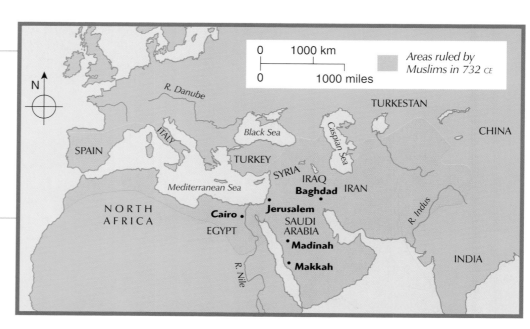

This map shows how far Islam had spread by the year 732 CE.

By the time the fourth khalifah, Ali, died in 661 CE, Islam had spread to Egypt, and along the coast of North Africa. Within 100 years of Muhammad's death, countries as far apart as Spain and India were ruled by Muslims.

The spread of Islam

When Islam was spreading to other countries, soldiers went first, but Muslim traders soon followed. They became well known for being honest and for living good lives. Sometimes this meant that other people decided they wanted to become Muslims, too. In this way, Islam became an important world religion very early in its history.

The Great Mosque in Cordoba, Spain

The Great Mosque in Cordoba was built by Muslims in the ninth century. It is a fine example of Muslim architecture. Since the thirteenth century, the building has been a church.

The prayer room in the Great Mosque in Cordoba, Spain.

Different groups in Islam

After Muhammad died, not all Muslims were happy with the choice of Abu Bakr as the new **khalifah** (leader). Some Muslims wanted Ali, Muhammad's son-in-law, to be leader. The disagreement carried on for many years.

Gradually, two groups formed. The group who supported Abu Bakr wanted each leader to be chosen by other Muslims. They were called the Sunni group. The second group, who supported Ali, wanted all leaders to come from Muhammad's family. This group was called the Shi'at Ali. Today we call this group Shi'ah Muslims.

Shi'ah Muslims

Most Shi'ah Muslims today live in Iraq and Iran. They are very strict Muslims. Some Shi'ah groups believe that they should fight for what is right, even if this means being killed themselves. Islam teaches that someone who dies for what they believe will go straight to be with **Allah** in **Paradise**. Some Muslims believe that giving up their life is worth it because their reward after death will be so great.

Sunni Muslims

About 90 per cent of all Muslims today belong to the group called Sunnis. Like Shi'ah Muslims, Sunni Muslims believe that they follow the teachings of Muhammad. They believe that the **Qur'an** shows the way that Muslims should live.

*This hand shape is a **symbol** for Shi'ah Muslims. They use it to remember Muhammad's family.*

Shi'ah Muslim men at the festival of Ashura.

Imams

Both Sunni and Shi'ah Muslims follow all the teachings of Islam. They respect the teachings of Muslim leaders, who are called **imams**.

For Shi'ah Muslims, 'imam' has a special meaning. They believe that there were twelve imams who had special powers. They were all members of the family of Muhammad. The first imam was Ali, who was the fourth khalifah. Ali passed the special power to his son, and so on. The twelfth imam disappeared in 880 CE, but Shi'ah Muslims believe that one day he will come back. Until then, teachers called **Ayatollahs** lead the Shi'ah Muslims.

The festival of Ashura

Every year, many Shi'ah Muslims meet at a place called Karbala. This is where the body of Husain, one of Muhammad's grandsons, was buried. The festival of Ashura remembers how Husain and his family were killed in battle. It is a chance for Shi'ah Muslims to think about evil in the world, and to promise to try to improve things.

How Muhammad received the Qur'an

This boy is sitting in the cave where Muslims believe that Muhammad had his first revelation.

Muslims believe that the **Qur'an** is a collection of messages from **Allah**. They believe that they were given to Muhammad by the **angel** Jibril. Muslims believe that the words were revealed (shown) to Muhammad in a special way at different times. These times are called the **revelations**.

The first revelation

Muslims teach that Muhammad went to a cave outside Makkah to be alone to think and to pray. He said afterwards that he saw the angel Jibril coming towards him, carrying a roll of silk material. Words were written on the silk in burning letters.

The angel told Muhammad to read the words, but Muhammad said that he could not. The angel told him three times, and at last Muhammad was able to read the words. The first words he read were: 'Recite! In the name of your Lord.'

Muslims believe that Muhammad received messages from Allah all his life. Sometimes he saw the angel Jibril again. Sometimes, he heard the messages inside his head.

Receiving the messages

When the messages were coming, Muhammad would lie down. He said that receiving the messages always made him feel close to death. He often became very hot, and would sweat a great deal. When he sat up afterwards, he was back to normal. He immediately repeated the message he had been given to his family and some friends, so that everyone would remember it, and nothing would be lost or forgotten.

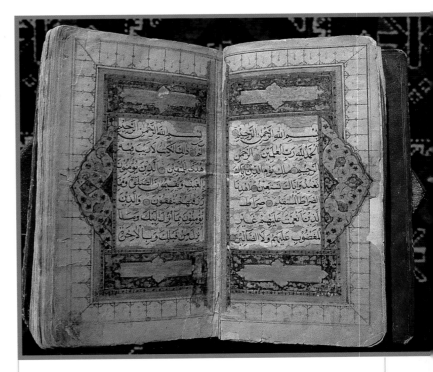

 This copy of the Qur'an was written by hand. It is more than 200 years old.

What Muslims believe about the Qur'an

Muslims believe that the words of the Qur'an come from Allah, so they should not be changed in any way. When the Qur'an is used for worship, it is always written in **Arabic**, the language Muhammad spoke. Muslims believe that the words of the Qur'an are Allah's final message to the world.

Translations

*The language of the Qur'an is Arabic. Arabic letters are very different from the letters used in English. Sometimes different spellings are used for the same sound. For example, Muhammad, Mahomet and Mohamed are all spellings used for the name of the **prophet**. The spellings used in this book are the ones that give the closest sound to the Arabic word.*

The Qur'an

The **Qur'an** is made up of chapters called **surahs**. There are 114 surahs altogether. The longest is surah 2, which has 286 verses. The shortest is surah 103, which has only three verses. Except for surah 9, each surah begins with the words: 'In the name of **Allah** the gracious, the merciful.'

▲ *The first two surahs in a beautifully decorated Qur'an.*

Muslims believe that the words of the Qur'an are exactly as they were given to Muhammad. When he received a **revelation**, Muhammad repeated the words to his family and friends, and they learnt them too. This was how important things were remembered in those days. The complete Qur'an was written down within 20 years of Muhammad's death. It has never been changed since.

Translations

When they worship together, Muslims always read the Qur'an in **Arabic**. However, there are millions of Muslims who do not speak Arabic very well. For them, the Qur'an has been translated into more than 40 other languages. Muslims believe that no translation can ever be completely exact, so all Muslims know at least some of the original Arabic words of the Qur'an.

Hafiz

Muslims believe that the Qur'an is the most important book that has ever been written. This is why some Muslims learn the whole book off by heart. Muslims who have done this are allowed to use the title **hafiz** as part of their name. They are very respected by other Muslims. Learning the Qur'an like this also makes sure that the Qur'an can never be lost. There will always be Muslims who can remember what it said, and could write the words down again.

How Muslims treat the Qur'an

Muslims treat the Qur'an with great respect. They do not eat, drink or speak while it is being read. It is usually placed on a special stool to be read. It is never allowed to touch the ground. When it is put away, it is always placed on the highest shelf, and wrapped in a special cloth. Nothing is ever placed on top of it.

Learning to read the Qur'an is very important to Muslims.

What the Qur'an says

These words from the Qur'an show the sort of teaching it gives:
I am close to them; I listen to the prayer of every seeker who calls to me. Listen to my call and believe in me, that you may walk in the right way. (Surah 2 186)

Muslim worship

Muslims believe that everything they do is part of their worship, because they have given their lives to **Allah**. This means that they try to live in a way which will follow the teachings of the **Qur'an** and of Islam.

▲ *Life at home and being part of a family is important to Muslims.*

The five pillars of Islam

The five pillars of Islam are the foundation of the way Muslims live. They are called pillars because they support the religion in the same way that a pillar supports a building. Muslims believe that keeping the five pillars helps them to follow their religion properly.

Halal and haram food

*Muslims believe that food comes from Allah. Islam has rules about foods which can and cannot be eaten. Food which Muslims can eat is **halal**. Food which they cannot eat is **haram**. Muslims may eat all fruit, grains and vegetables. Meat from fish, poultry, sheep, goats and camels is also allowed, but the animal has to be killed in a special way so that it does not suffer. Any food which comes from a pig is haram. The rules about which foods can and cannot be eaten are given in the Qur'an.*

The first pillar of Islam is the **Shahadah**, the Declaration of Faith. This says: 'There is no God but Allah and Muhammad is the messenger of Allah.' The second pillar is **salah**, which says that Muslims should pray five times a day. The third pillar is **zakah**, which means giving money to people who are poor or in need. The fourth pillar is **sawm**, which means **fasting**. Every year, during the month of **Ramadan**, Muslims fast during the hours of daylight. The fifth pillar is **Hajj**. This is the **pilgrimage** to Makkah, which every Muslim tries to make at least once in their life.

Worship in the home

Muslim families read the Qur'an together at home, and children are brought up to treat it with respect. Most Muslims have pictures of important **mosques** or of places in Makkah on the walls. They do not have any pictures of people or animals connected with Islam, as these are not allowed.

Muslims do not drink alcohol. It is a drug that can harm the body. Alcohol is not allowed in Muslim countries. For the same reasons, Muslims should not smoke cigarettes.

Muslims eat only food which is halal, because they believe this is what Allah wants.

Worship in a mosque

The most important part of Muslim worship is prayer. All Muslims pray five times a day, at times which are given in the **Qur'an**. This is **salah**. The five times of prayer are between first light and when the sun rises, after noon, between mid-afternoon and sunset, after sunset but before it is dark, and while it is dark. The most important prayers are those after noon on a Friday. At that time, Muslim men are expected to go to the **mosque**. Women may also go to the mosque, but if not, they pray at home.

When Muslims pray, they always face towards the holy city of Makkah. In a mosque, a special part of the wall, called the **mihrab**, shows where Makkah is. If they are travelling, Muslims sometimes carry a special compass to show the direction of Makkah from wherever they are in the world. Muslims can pray in any clean place. They often use a special mat to kneel on when they pray.

Wudu

Before they pray, Muslims wash themselves. This is a special washing called **wudu**. Wudu makes them ready to talk to **Allah**, who is holy. It gives them time to forget what they have been doing, and to focus on Allah. Wudu has nothing to do with being clean or dirty.

All Muslims perform wudu before they pray.

Prayers

Muslim prayers follow a set pattern of movements, called a **rak'ah**. The number of rak'ahs in the prayers changes at different prayer times. A rak'ah includes a number of different movements. The movements are standing, bowing, kneeling and touching the ground with the forehead. Prayers are said in each position. For the last movement, people turn their heads from side to side to remember the two **angels** that Muslims believe are always with every person.

In their prayers, Muslims say thank you to Allah that they can worship him. They also pray for Muhammad and for all Muslims everywhere. Private prayers, using their own words, can be added at the end of a rak'ah, or made at any other time.

A Muslim prayer

As part of their prayers, Muslims repeat the first words of the Qur'an:

All praise be to Allah,
the Lord of the universe,
the most merciful,
the most kind,
*Master of the **Day of Judgement**,*
You alone do we worship,
From you alone do we seek help.
Show us the next step along the straight path of those earning your favour.

At the end of the last rak'ah everyone looks from side to side, to greet the two angels they believe are with each person.

The mosque

*A mosque does not have to be a building. This is the **mihrab** of an open-air mosque in Jerusalem.*

Muslims believe that they can worship **Allah** in any place that is clean. Like many religions, they also have special buildings for worship. These buildings are called **mosques**. (Sometimes the Arabic name **masjid** is used.)

What is a mosque?

A mosque can be any place where Muslims worship. The **Qur'an** says that there should be a mosque whenever 40 Muslim men live in the same area. Some mosques are very old and beautiful. Some mosques are specially built, but some are in houses or other buildings. They do not have to be indoors. In hot countries, a mosque may be just a piece of sand marked with an arrow to show the direction of Makkah. At home, many Muslims have a room or part of a room which they always use for prayer.

What happens in a mosque?

The main room in a mosque is used for prayers. In larger mosques, there is a room for women to pray. Otherwise, women pray separately from the men, at the back of the main room. Mosques are also used for a school called the **madrasah**. From the age of four, children attend the madrasah to learn **Arabic** and the Qur'an. Other rooms at the mosque may be used for meetings.

Parts of a mosque

Specially built mosques usually have a **dome**. This helps to make a feeling of space inside the mosque. There is usually at least one tall tower, called a **minaret**. Years ago, the top of the minaret was where the **mu'adhin** stood to make the Call to Prayer. The Call to Prayer is made by the mu'adhin five times a day. It tells all Muslims in the area that it is time to pray.

All mosques must have a place where people can wash before they pray. This is **wudu**, the special washing done before Muslims talk to Allah. Some mosques have a pool or a fountain outside for wudu. Modern mosques have special washrooms with rows of taps. Men and women wash separately.

The Call to Prayer

*The Call to Prayer is called the **adhan**. It says:*
'God is the greatest. There is no God but Allah. Muhammad is the prophet of Allah. Come to prayer, come to security, Allah is most great!'

For the first prayers of the day, the adhan also includes the words 'Prayer is better than sleep.'

A mu'adhin making the Call to Prayer, called the adhan.

Inside a mosque

You can find the places mentioned in this book on the map on page 44.

The prayer room

The main room of a **mosque** is the prayer room. This has no furniture, but the floor is always covered with carpet or special prayer mats. Usually there is a pattern on the carpet to help people to pray in neat rows, and to find the direction of Makkah. Nobody coming to worship has a particular place, because everyone is equal in front of **Allah**, so it does not matter if they pray at the front or the back of the mosque. Everyone takes off their shoes before they go into the prayer room. This shows respect, and keeps the mosque clean for prayer.

The mihrab

In every mosque there is an arch or a special part of one wall which shows the direction of Makkah. This is called the **mihrab**. It is often beautifully decorated. The person leading the prayers usually stands in front of the mihrab.

The minbar

At the front of a mosque, usually on the right of the mihrab, is the **minbar**. This is a part of the floor which is higher than the rest. It is often at the top of a few steps. The **imam** uses the minbar when he talks to Muslims at the prayers on a Friday. Everyone in the mosque can then see and hear him clearly.

This is the mihrab in the Mosque of the Prophet, in Madinah.

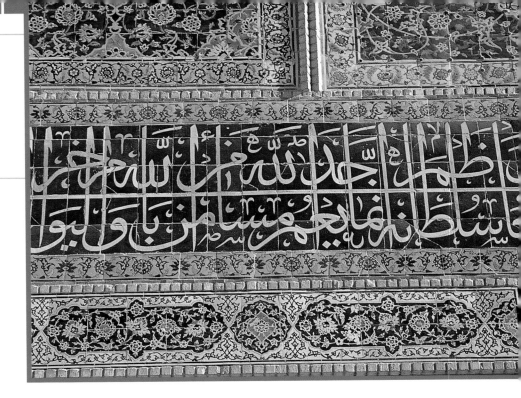

This calligraphy is part of the decoration on the wall of a mosque in Iran.

The imam

The imam is a leader chosen by all the other Muslims at the mosque. They choose him because they respect him and because he knows the **Qur'an** very well. The imam teaches them about the Qur'an and about their lives as Muslims.

Decorations

There are never any pictures or statues inside a mosque. This is because Muhammad was afraid that some people might worship them instead of Allah. Instead, mosques are beautifully decorated with patterns and words from the Qur'an. Carpets are often made in lovely rich colours. Green is popular because it was Muhammad's favourite colour, and a rich turquoise blue is often used too.

Calligraphy

A special form of decoration used in mosques and other places is called calligraphy. This is the art of beautiful handwriting. It began when people writing out parts of the Qur'an wanted to make the writing as beautiful as possible. Sometimes it can be used to make pictures out of letters.

25

Places of worship

The Ka'bah

You can find the places mentioned in this book on the map on page 44.

The **Ka'bah** is the most important place in the world for Muslims. It is in the Great **Mosque** in Makkah. It is so old that no one knows how old it is. The Ka'bah was very old even when Muhammad was alive. Muslims believe that it was the first place in the world where **Allah** was worshipped.

The Ka'bah is built of brick in the shape of a cube. It is 15 metres long, 10 metres wide and 14 metres high. Inside, it is a room covered with words from the **Qur'an**. During the time of the **Hajj** (**pilgrimage**), the Ka'bah is covered with black cloths which are beautifully embroidered in gold thread with the words of the Qur'an. At the end of the Hajj this cloth is cut up and pilgrims can take small pieces home with them.

The Black Stone

In one corner of the Ka'bah is the Black Stone. It is probably a **meteorite**, and it is the oldest and most important part of the Ka'bah. Today it is in a silver frame. Pilgrims on Hajj try to get close enough to touch or kiss the Black Stone.

There are many stories about the Black Stone. One of them says that when Muhammad was young, the Black Stone was removed while the Ka'bah was being repaired. A quarrel broke out among the leaders of Makkah about who was important enough to put it back in its place. Muhammad settled the quarrel by lifting the stone onto a rug. The leaders took a corner of the rug each, so they could all carry it. Muslims say it is because of events like this that Muhammad was so respected.

The Black Stone is the oldest part of the Ka'bah.

The Mosque of the Dome of the Rock

The Mosque of the Dome of the Rock is in Jerusalem. Jerusalem is the third holiest city in the world for Muslims, after Makkah and Madinah. The Mosque of the Dome of the Rock is one of the most beautiful mosques in the world. It was built in the seventh century CE. Many Muslims believe that it was from here that Muhammad was taken to heaven on the **Night of the Journey**. They also believe that it is from this spot that the call to judgement will be made on the **Day of Judgement** at the end of the world.

Inside the Mosque of the Dome of the Rock.

The Day of Judgement

Muslims believe that the Day of Judgement will be the end of the world. It will be announced from the Dome of the Rock in Jerusalem. Islam teaches that on that day the seas will boil and mountains will crumble to dust. People will be judged on how they have lived on earth.

The Hajj

Every Muslim who has good health and enough money is expected to go on a **pilgrimage** to Makkah at least once in their life. This pilgrimage is called **Hajj**. To be a proper Hajj, the person must be in Makkah between 8 and 13 Dhul-Hijjah. This is the last month of the Muslim year. About two million Muslims go to Makkah at that time.

Pilgrims wearing the special clothes called ihram.

What do pilgrims do on Hajj?

All pilgrims do the same things on Hajj. These include walking quickly round the **Ka'bah** seven times and hurrying seven times between two small hills near the Ka'bah. They also drink water from the Well of Zamzam in the grounds of the Great **Mosque** in Makkah.

The wuquf

The **wuquf** is the most important part of Hajj. Wuquf means: 'Stand before Allah'. Pilgrims travel to the Plain of Arafat near Makkah, and stand and pray there from noon until sunset. They ask **Allah** to forgive them for everything they have done wrong in their life. They believe that if they are really sorry, Allah will forgive them.

On the morning of 10 Dhul-Hijjah, pilgrims travel a few kilometres to Mina. They throw stones at three pillars. This reminds them of the story in the **Qur'an** about how Ibrahim drove away the devil who was tempting him.

After the first pillar has been stoned, the pilgrims sacrifice a sheep or goat. This is part of the festival of Id-ul-Adha in which Muslims all over the world take part. After the animal has been sacrificed, male pilgrims either cut their hair or shave it off altogether. Women cut a lock of their hair. They camp at Mina for three more days, then they return to Makkah. They walk around the Ka'bah again, and then drink more water from the Well of Zamzam. When they have done this, their Hajj has ended.

Why do people go on Hajj?

Going on Hajj is a chance to worship with millions of other Muslims. Muslims believe that the most important thing is that they should go on Hajj in the right way. Then Allah will forgive them everything they have done wrong in their life.

Pilgrims on Hajj camp near Makkah.

Ihram

*On Hajj, Muslims are expected to behave in a special way called **ihram**. They live very simply and wear simple clothes, also called ihram. All the men wear two sheets of white cotton. One is wrapped around the lower part of their body, and the other goes over their left shoulder. Wearing the same clothes shows that Allah cares equally for everyone. Women do not usually wear special clothes.*

Celebrating Ramadan

At sunset during Ramadan, Muslims usually break their fast with a snack.

Every year during the month of **Ramadan**, Muslims **fast** during the hours of daylight. This means they do not eat or drink anything all day. This is very hard, but Muslims believe that it is important. Special charts are printed with lists of the times in different places when the sun rises and sets, so people know exactly when to stop eating. Before sunrise, they usually have a meal which provides lots of energy, and then they eat nothing until the sun sets, when they have a light snack. A main meal follows later, after the evening prayer.

Why do Muslims fast?

Muslims fast because **Allah** says in the **Qur'an** that they should. It is a way of showing that they are living as Allah wants. Muslims believe it shows that Islam is the most important thing in their lives. They also believe it shows that everyone is equal. Hunger is the same whether someone is rich or poor.

Who fasts?

Ramadan is hard, but it is not meant to be cruel. Very young children do not fast, and children over the age of seven do not usually fast as strictly as grown-ups. Anyone who is travelling does not have to fast, but they are expected to make up the days they have missed later.

Women who are having a baby and people who are ill are not expected to fast. If someone has an illness which means that going without food could be dangerous, they are expected to pay some money to the poor instead of fasting.

What happens to a Muslim who does not fast?

Muslims believe that Allah expects people to fast, and that if they do not, they are cheating him. They believe that at the end of the world, there will be a **Day of Judgement**. On this day, Muslims teach, Allah will judge everyone on how they have lived. Each person will get the reward or punishment they deserve.

The Muslim calendar

Islam follows a lunar year. This means that every month begins when there is a new moon, so each month lasts 29 or 30 days. Each Muslim year is about 10 days shorter than a 'Western' year. This means that Muslim months are not at the same time every year.

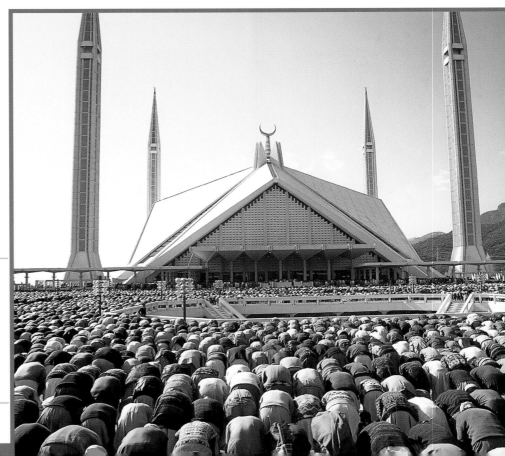

*Prayers at a **mosque** in Pakistan during Ramadan.*

Celebrating Id-ul-Fitr and Id-ul-Adha

Id (sometimes spelled Eid), is the Muslim word for festival. Id-ul-Fitr is the festival which ends **Ramadan**, the month when Muslims **fast**. Muslims look forward to it very much. Before the festival begins, everyone gives money to the poor. This is called Zakat-ul-Fitr. The idea is that everyone should have enough money to be able to celebrate the festival properly.

On the night that Ramadan ends, many Muslims do not go to bed. Instead, they meet friends outside, and watch the sky together to see the new moon. When it appears, everyone is in holiday mood and rushes to greet each other. They wish each other 'Happy Id'.

At Id-ul-Fitr, everyone wears new clothes or their best clothes. There are special services at the **mosque** or at a place where large numbers of Muslims can meet. Thousands of people may gather together to celebrate the festival. Id-ul-Fitr is a chance for people who have not seen each other for a long time to meet and talk. There are parties, and people exchange presents. In Muslim countries Id-ul-Fitr is a three-day holiday.

At Id-ul-Fitr everyone wears new clothes or their best clothes.

At Id-ul-Adha, pilgrims on Hajj shave their heads.

Id-ul-Adha

Id-ul-Adha is the most important festival of the Muslim year. It forms part of the **Hajj**, but it is celebrated by Muslims all over the world. Id-ul-Adha means Festival of Sacrifice. The most important part of Id-ul-Adha is sacrificing an animal – a sheep, goat, cow or camel.

A Muslim man should know how to kill an animal for sacrifice so that it does not suffer, and so that the meat from it is **halal**. In Western countries, killing an animal at home is against the law, so the killing is done in an abattoir by someone who is specially trained. The meat from the animal is divided up, and one part is always given to the poor.

Ibrahim's sacrifice
*At Id-ul-Adha, Muslims remember the story in the **Qur'an** about how Ibrahim was asked to sacrifice his son, Isma'il. This was a test of obedience to **Allah**. Ibrahim did not have to kill Isma'il, because as he was about to make the sacrifice he was told to sacrifice a ram instead.*

Celebrating other festivals

You can find the places mentioned in this book on the map on page 44.

Id-ul-Adha and Id-ul-Fitr are the most important Muslim festivals, but there are other days which are also important.

The Day of the Hijrah (1 Muharram)

This is the Muslim New Year's Day, which is celebrated on 1 Muharram, the first month of the Muslim year. It remembers the **hijrah**, Muhammad's journey to Madinah. Muslims believe that this event was very important, because it was the beginning of the success of Islam. Muslim years take their number from the year of the hijrah, so they are counted as years after the hijrah – 'AH'.

The Night of the Journey (27 Rajab)

Muslims believe that on this night Muhammad made a miraculous journey with the **angel** Jibril. They rode from Makkah to Jerusalem on the back of a horse with wings. From the place where the **Mosque** of the Dome of the Rock now stands, Muhammad was taken to heaven. He met and prayed with all the **prophets**. Then **Allah** himself taught Muhammad about the importance of praying five times a day (**salah**). Some Muslims believe that this was a **vision**, and others believe that Muhammad did visit heaven.

Inside a beautiful mosque in the Yemen.

*An old painting showing the **Night of the Journey**. Notice that you cannot see Muhammad's face. Muslims believe that to show his face would be an insult to Allah and Islam.*

The Night of Power (27 Ramadan)

This is when Muslims remember the time when Muhammad received his first **revelation** of the **Qur'an**. No one knows exactly when this happened, but it is usually celebrated on 27 **Ramadan**. Many Muslims spend all night reading the Qur'an and thinking about why it is important for them. In some places, groups of friends meet and spend all night going to pray in different mosques.

For Muslims, festivals are not just occasions for worshipping Allah, but also for putting right things that are wrong in their life. They are a time to remember the rest of the Muslim family all over the world.

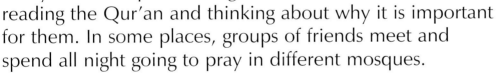

Zakah

*Giving to people who are in need is part of a Muslim's duty. It is a special part of most festivals. This is called **Zakah** (or **Zakat**). Zakah is the third of the five pillars of Islam. Giving Zakah reminds Muslims that everything comes from Allah.*

3 5

Special occasions – childhood

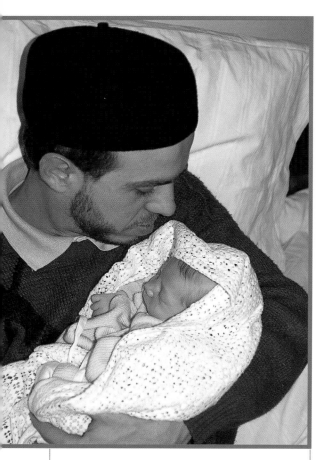

The Call to Prayer is whispered to a newborn baby.

Muslims believe that children are a gift from **Allah**. Muslims regard it as the duty of parents to bring their children up to become good Muslims.

When a baby is born, he or she is washed, and dressed or wrapped in a shawl. Then the baby is given to the head of the family. He whispers the Call to Prayer and the Command to Worship in its ear. Muslims believe that this welcomes the baby into the family of Islam as soon as it is born, and it means that the first word the baby hears is 'Allah'.

Aqiqah

The ceremony called **aqiqah** is held when the baby is seven days old. Friends and relatives come to a feast, and the baby is given its name. Then its head is shaved. The hair which is cut off is weighed, and money is given to the poor. The amount of money given is what the hair would be worth if it was made of silver. Even if the baby was born with very little or no hair, money is still given to the poor.

Muslim names

Choosing the name for a baby is an important duty for Muslim parents. Sometimes an old family name is used. Sometimes the name of Muhammad or one of his family is chosen. A common choice for boys is one of the 99 names of Allah given in the **Qur'an**, with 'Abd' in front of it. Abd means 'servant of' in **Arabic**. This is a way of saying that the boy will be Allah's servant.

Bismillah

Some Muslim children have a ceremony called **bismillah** at about the time they are four years old. Bismillah means 'In the name of Allah.' At bismillah, the child learns words from the Qur'an. These words are at the beginning of every **surah** in the Qur'an: 'In the name of Allah, the Gracious, the Merciful.' The child learns how to say each Arabic word correctly, and is taught how to pray. Even if they do not have this ceremony, all Muslim children from about the age of four are expected to attend the **madrasah** at the **mosque**. This is so that they can learn Arabic and about Islam.

The 99 names of Allah

In the Qur'an there are 99 names for Allah. They all describe what Allah is like. Some of the names are: the eternal, the creator, the mighty, the generous, the gracious, the kind, the forgiver, the merciful, the wise one, the holy one.

▼ *Children go to the madrasah to learn about Islam.*

Special occasions – marriage

For Muslims, marriage is very important. Because marriage joins two families, Muslims believe that it should involve the whole family as well as the couple. Many Muslim marriages are 'arranged'. This means that older relatives suggest a suitable marriage partner. Muslim law forbids forced marriages.

A Muslim wedding group in London.

Marrying more than one person

When Muhammad was alive, a man could marry as many women as he wanted. The **Qur'an** says that a man should marry no more than four wives. He must treat them all exactly the same. Most people today agree that this is impossible, so most men only marry one wife. In Western countries, it is against the law to be married to more than one person at the same time.

The marriage

A Muslim wedding is simple. The couple make promises in front of witnesses. There are readings from the Qur'an, and prayers. Before the wedding takes place, the couple agree rules for the marriage. These are written down, and the couple sign them. The rules include things they both believe are necessary for their marriage. Signing the rules may take place months or even years before the couple begin to live together.

The wedding party or **walimah** takes place within three days of the couple beginning to live together. It is usually a feast for friends and relatives. In some countries, the walimah is a huge party which lasts for days. Muhammad did not approve of this, especially if it meant that families were short of money afterwards.

Divorce

Divorce is the ending of a marriage while the husband and wife are still alive. Muslims do not approve of divorce. Friends and relatives try to help a couple whose marriage is in trouble. There must also be a wait of at least three months. This gives time for the couple to think again. However, Islam teaches that if the marriage has really failed, there is no point in the couple staying together. Once the divorce is final, an ex-husband does not have any responsibility for his wife. Men and women can marry again after divorce.

▲ A Muslim bride wearing traditional dress.

Who can a Muslim marry?

A Muslim woman may only marry a Muslim. A Muslim man may marry a Muslim, a Christian or a Jew. If a Muslim man wishes to marry a member of any other religion, the woman must become a Muslim first.

Death and beyond

Muslims do not believe that it is right for anyone to be on their own when they die. If someone is known to be dying, relatives and friends gather round the bed. If they can speak, the person says they are sorry for anything they have done which has hurt people. They ask **Allah** to forgive them, too. Then they repeat the **Shahadah**: 'There is no God except Allah, and Muhammad is the prophet of Allah.' If the person cannot speak, their relatives say this for them.

When the person has died, their body is washed and wrapped in a white cloth. Muslims think it is better if this is done by relatives. If the person has been on **Hajj** to Makkah, their body is wrapped in the **ihram** cloth they wore for the **pilgrimage**.

Muslim funerals

Muslims believe that funerals should be simple. Death happens to everyone, no matter how much money they have, so it is not right to spend a lot of money on a funeral.

▲ *A funeral service at Regent's Park **Mosque** in London.*

When Muslims die they are always buried. They are never **cremated**. Muslims believe that a body should be buried so that the head is turned towards Makkah. The person's name may be put on a simple headstone.

▲ *A Muslim graveyard in Pakistan.*

After death

Muslims believe that when someone dies, their **soul** waits for the **Day of Judgement**. This will be at the end of the world. Those who followed Allah and asked his forgiveness while they were alive for things they did wrong will go to join him in **Paradise**. This will be a garden of happiness. Muslims believe that people who did not believe in Allah while they were alive will go to burn in **hell**.

Angels, messengers from Allah

*Muslims believe that every person has two special **angels** with them all the time. They keep a record of everything – good and bad – that the person does in their life. This record will be given to the person on the Day of Judgement. (There will be no need to give the record to Allah because Allah knows everything.) Muslims greet these angels at the end of their prayers by looking from side to side after the last **rak'ah**.*

Ways to be a Muslim

The Muslim family

Family life is very important to Muslims. Islam teaches that parents have a duty to care for their children. It also teaches that when the parents are old, their children have a duty to look after them. Old people have had more experience of life, so their opinions should be respected.

Muslims believe very strongly that Muslims all over the world belong to one family. It does not matter where they live, which language they speak or the colour of their skin. Caring for other members of the Muslim family is important, especially if they live in a poorer country.

Clothes

Islam teaches that both men and women should dress decently. For men, this means being covered from the waist to the knees. For women, the head, arms and legs should be covered. Outside the home, many Muslim women dress so that as little as possible of their body can be seen. They wear a full length dress over their other clothes, and a veil over their head. This style of clothing is called **hijab**.

Caring for children is part of a parent's duty.

Many Muslim women choose to stay at home to care for their family.

Work

Islam teaches that work is necessary and important. A job should be done as well as possible. The work should not go against the teachings of Islam. The woman's job is usually to care for the home and children. The man's job is to go out and earn money so that the woman can do this properly. Some Muslim women do work outside the home, but many feel that making a loving home for their family is the most important job they could ever do.

Ways to live

*Islam teaches that there are five sorts of actions. Some things must be done (e.g. prayer), some should be done, some should not be done and some are forbidden (e.g. worshipping **idols**). A fifth group includes most everyday actions, when each person decides for themselves what is right by reading the **Qur'an** and Muhammad's teachings.*

Map

The globe on the right shows the location of the map below.

This map shows some places that are important in the history of Islam.

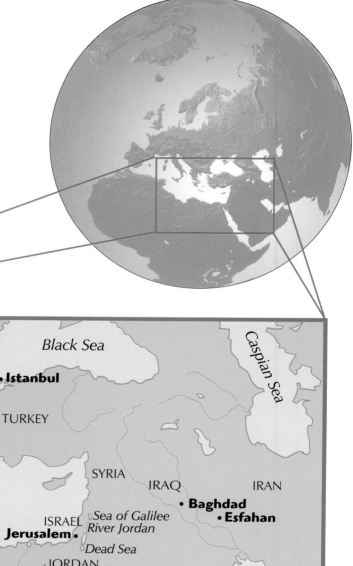

ITALY

Black Sea

•**Istanbul**

GREECE

TURKEY

Caspian Sea

Mediterranean Sea

SYRIA

IRAQ

IRAN

•**Baghdad**

•**Esfahan**

ISRAEL

Sea of Galilee

River Jordan

Jerusalem•

Dead Sea

JORDAN

EGYPT

Persian Gulf

River Nile

Red Sea

•**Madinah**

SAUDI ARABIA

•**Makkah**

N

0   500 km

0   500 miles

Place names
Some places on this map can be spelled in different ways:
Esfahan – Isfahan   Madinah (or al–Madinah) – Medina
Makkah – Mecca

Timechart

Major events in World history

BCE **3000–1700** Indus valley civilization (Hinduism)

c2685–1196 Egyptian civilization

c2000 Abraham lived (Judaism)

1800 Stonehenge completed

c528 Siddhattha Buddha born (Buddhism)

c450–146 Greek Empire

200 Great Wall of China begun

c300–300CE Roman Empire

c4 Jesus of Nazareth born (Christianity)

CE **570** Muhammad born (Islam)

1066 Battle of Hastings and the Norman conquest of England

1325–1521 Aztec Empire

1400 Black Death kills one person in three in China, North Africa and Europe

1469 Guru Nanak born (Sikhism)

1564 William Shakespeare born

1914–18 World War I

1939–45 World War II

1946 First computer invented

1969 First moon landings

2000 Millennium celebrations all over the world

Major events in Islamic history

CE **570** Birth of Muhammad

595 Muhammad marries Khadijah

610 Muhammad receives first revelation from the angel Jibril

622 The hijrah

632 Muhammad dies

637 Muslims gain control of Jerusalem

644–656 Khalifah Uthman orders that the complete Qur'an be written down

680 Husain killed (remembered by Shi'ah Muslims at the festival of Ashura)

690s Mosque of the Dome of the Rock completed

711 Muslims conquer Spain

762–766 Baghdad built (then the largest city on earth)

1520–1566 Suleiman the Magnificent (great Muslim leader)

1857 British capture of Delhi ends 1000 years of Muslim rule in India

1947 Pakistan created as a Muslim country in the Indian sub-continent

1979 Establishment of the Islamic Republic of Iran

Glossary

adhan	the Call to Prayer
Allah	Muslim name for God
angel	messenger from God
aqiqah	ceremony in which a Muslim child is given its name
Arabic	language spoken by Arabs, and used for Muslim worship
Ayatollah	teacher of Shi'ah Muslims
bismillah	first words of the Qur'an (also a ceremony for children)
cremate	burn a body after death
Day of Judgement	end of the world when Allah will judge everyone
dome	a shape like half a ball
eternal	lasting for ever
fast	go without food and drink
hafiz	title given to someone who has learned the whole of the Qur'an by heart
Hajj	pilgrimage to Makkah
halal	allowed (food that Muslims can eat)
haram	not allowed (food that Muslims cannot eat)
hijab	'veil' (used to describe the clothing worn by some Muslim women)
hijrah	Muhammad's journey to Madinah
hell	place of everlasting punishment for life after death
idol	statue worshipped as a god
ihram	the special way of living and the clothes worn by pilgrims on Hajj
imam	Muslim leader and teacher
Ka'bah	the most important Muslim shrine

khalifah	one of the first leaders of Islam
madrasah	school at the mosque
masjid	Arabic name for a Muslim place of worship
meteorite	rock-like object that falls from space
mihrab	arch that shows the direction of Makkah
minaret	tall tower of a mosque
minbar	platform in a mosque, used for teaching
mosque	Muslim place of worship
mu'adhin	man who calls Muslims to prayer
Night of the Journey	night on which Muhammad made his miraculous journey to heaven
Paradise	garden of happiness for life after death
pilgrimage	journey made for religious reasons
prophet	someone who tells people what God wants
Qur'an	Muslim holy book
rak'ah	positions for Muslim prayers
Ramadan	ninth month of the Muslim year, when Muslims fast
revelation	something shown (times when Muhammad was given the Qur'an)
salah	prayer five times a day
sawm	fasting
Shahadah	the summing up of the most important Muslim beliefs
soul	the part of a person that lives forever
surah	chapter of the Qur'an
symbol	something that stands for something else
vision	religious experience which feels like a dream
walimah	wedding party
wudu	washing before prayer
wuquf	'Stand before Allah', the most important part of Hajj
zakah (or zakat)	giving to the poor

Index

Titles in the *Religions of the World* series include:

Hardback   0 431 14953 4

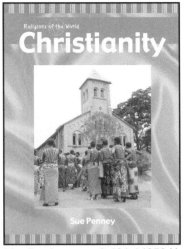

Hardback   0 431 14950 X

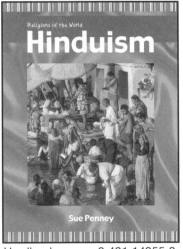

Hardback   0 431 14955 0

Hardback   0 431 14952 6

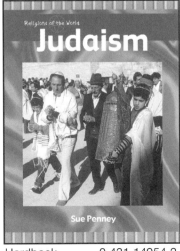

Hardback   0 431 14954 2

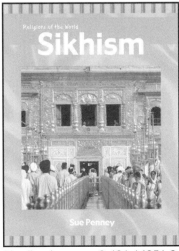

Hardback   0 431 14951 8

Find out about the other titles in this series on our website www.heinemann.co.uk/library